GRACE
of GRATITUDE
REFLECTIONS

*Thoughts to inspire you
on your daily path*

DEBORAH PERDUE

Grace of Gratitude Reflections
Copyright ©2015
All rights reserved.

No portion of this book may be reproduced by any means, electronic or mechanical, including photocopying, recording, or by any information storage retrieval system, without permission of the copyright's owner.

Published by
Applegate Valley Publishing
Grants Pass, Oregon
www.applegatevalleypublishing.com
www.graceofgratitude.com

ISBN #978-0-9827759-9-1

Design by Deborah Perdue of Illumination Graphics
www.illuminationgraphics.com

Cover Illustration by Tara Thelen
www.tara-artwork.com

*This pocket guide is created for you,
to be a source of inspiration and
encouragement during
your daily life, when you may need
a remembrance of all there is to be
grateful for.*

*I know that peace and joy expand by being
grateful, and I wish that for you.*

LIFE IS GOOD!

Deborah Perdue

MY DEEPEST GRATITUDE AND
APPRECIATION TO:

Tara Thelen, amazing artist extraordinaire,
my business partner and dear friend...

To all the readers of the Daily Gratitude
Affirmations I send out, especially the ones
who have let me know they appreciate my
thoughts, which prompted this book...

To my husband Peter
who is my steadfast partner,
grounding me when I am in need...

And to God
who, to me, is absolute love, and is within
everything, not some angry guy in the sky!

Saying "yes" is my natural inclination.
I say yes to more and more good in my life,
and in the world.

Peace and love and joy abide in my heart,
and for this and so much more,
I am deeply grateful!

From time to time, I subconsciously set up a conflict in my life that ends up helping me to grow into a more healed version of myself, by learning what it all means. It may seem as though another person is judging me which always feels terrible, or that I have done something wrong, so self-forgiveness is needed.

But at the core of the situation, it can be an opportunity to love myself more; to realize I need to stand up for myself more; and to help me be more of the Light and Love I came here to be.

I am thankful for all the growth opportunities in my life – so that I can become more fully the true me!

GRACE of GRATITUDE REFLECTIONS

So very thankful for the feelings
of comfort and calm.

Immersed in wondrous nature,
I hear the soothing sounds
of a river flowing by, or gentle waves
lapping on a bay,
in and out, in and out, reminding me
of the steadfast serenity
that is always to be found
deep within me,
no matter how tumultuous and busy
life may seem.

Breathing into the present moment,
I am thankful for peace and calm
soothing my soul tonight.

Sometimes, when very absorbed in the present moment, time stands still and then for an instant, I am transported out of day-to-day living, and get a glimpse into eternity. Ego dissolves, and I am in total joy and bliss, and time is suspended...

When I snap out of it, I realize that I have been away, almost out of body,
and I marvel at that feeling.
And this is an altered state, without drugs or alcohol!

I am thankful for this portal into other dimensions and for the reminder that I am much greater than my time here on earth in this body temple.
As we all are.

Grace *of* Gratitude Reflections

"The material world is but a fleeting shadow of the unseen."
– Myrtle Fillmore

Gratefully, I put stock in the unseen which overrides and negates all the seeming problems, evil and destruction of this world.

What is real is permanent, unchanging, and we can always go to this realm in our minds.

The unseen which animates everything is creativity, is power, is love, is the peace which passeth all understanding.

I am grateful to realize that what we can't see with our human eyes is much more real than what we can see.

Thank you, God.

Deborah Perdue

So very grateful for the abundant love that surrounds me:
shared with my birth family, in my marriage, in the myriad of like-minded friends I have,
so easily felt with our cherished dogs, and the ever-cheerful cockatiels.

And I am grateful for my own loving, caring, compassionate heart.

Love is the glue that holds us all together and we are always immersed in it, and permeated with it.

I am thankful for all the love everywhere!
Love abounds in this universe –
let me focus on that.

GRACE *of* GRATITUDE REFLECTIONS

Tonight I am so grateful for knowing that
everything happens for a reason
even when it is not immediately apparent
and that there is divine right timing and
order in all.

The universe is divinely orchestrated
and we are supported, guided and
sustained in every moment.

As I trust in Spirit's timing, not my own,
I let go and relax.

If we want love, be love.
If we want peace, be peace.

Although I know I falter sometimes, I do want more peace and love in this world, so I strive to be more loving and more filled with peace each and every day.

Unafraid, I let myself be vulnerable and seen.

I am a shining beacon of love, light and peace, and I am deeply grateful to stand strong and sure and steadfast
like a lighthouse, showing the way.

"I rejoice that I am not bound by the past."
Science of Mind magazine, July 2015

There is a wise saying by Ernest Holmes
"Principle is not bound by precedence."
This means that what has happened
before, even if it has "always" happened,
does not need to be our experience going
forward. What freedom there is
in that truth!

I am deeply grateful for a brand new day
with brand new opportunities,
and I am thankful for a brand new me,
with new ways of thinking.

Life is change; it is never stagnant
and I rejoice that this is so!

DEBORAH PERDUE

Gratitude washes over me today.
I am permeated with that lovely feeling
of enough,
of plenty, of all is well.

And I am deeply thankful.

GRACE *of* GRATITUDE REFLECTIONS

I am so thankful for vacations,
short or long,
to faraway exotic lands
or even staycations.

Vacations are a chance to let go
of all the to-dos and "shoulds"
of everyday life
and simply relax, lose track of time,
and enjoy...

Thank you, Spirit, for freedom, laziness
and fun!

I am so thankful for simplicity –
for the simple things in life
like eating, sleeping, waking and walking.
Like unconditionally loving
and petting my devoted dog
and watering my garden.

My head often wants to complicate things
and run ahead planning and plotting
but life can be simple if we allow it to be.

Grounded in gratitude, I let life be easy!

GRACE *of* GRATITUDE REFLECTIONS

*"I fairly sizzle with zeal and enthusiasm, and
spring forth with a mighty faith
to do the things that ought to be done by me."*
Charles Fillmore, founder of Unity
when he was 93 years old

I am deeply grateful for the wellspring of
ideas in my heart and soul,
for new beginnings, for stretching out of
mundane routines, knowing it is safe and
more than that, exciting!

Thank you, Spirit, for my own zest for life,
and exploring new horizons
when I am inspired.

I am grateful for the knowing that I am
doing everything just right;
that I am already perfect (as we all are)
exactly as I am, that if mistakes are made,
I can choose again and do it differently.

I am so grateful for loving myself just as I
am and just as I am not!

I am worthy beyond measure and part of
the Oneness of Spirit,
and I am thankful for remembering this,
when I slip back into
self-defeating old patterns.

GRACE *of* GRATITUDE REFLECTIONS

Deeply grateful for the beauty of
summertime!
for the light that starts
the mornings earlier...
for the light and sunshine
that sparkles all day...
for the beauty and bounty of gardens...
and for the light and love in my heart
today!

I am grateful for discovering
the power of thankfulness.
It is the elixir of life, the nectar
that changes a seemingly sour situation
to sweetness and light.

I celebrate what there is to be grateful for
in all things.

Even in grief or dire situations, I can find a
treasure of thanksgiving
if I look hard enough.

I bask in gratitude each and every day!

So thankful for each special person
in my life.
I deeply appreciate each connection,
whether fleeting or a mainstay in my life.

When a special person in my life
transitions, let me remember how much
I am grateful for the deep love in my life
that transcends time and space.

I am also grateful to know that nothing
and nobody really dies
and that I will be reunited with loved ones
on the other side.

I take the time each day to let my loved
ones know I care, realizing that is what
really matters.

Change is always in the air!

I am grateful for all the changes that
happen in my life, each and every day.
Used to be I was resistant to change, and
that doesn't really serve me, as change is
the one constant, the one thing that we
can depend on besides love.
So, I am thankful for my ability and
willingness to roll with change.

Thank you, Spirit,
for the ever-changing conditions and
situations that keep shape shifting
so that life never becomes boring!

GRACE *of* GRATITUDE REFLECTIONS

I am so thankful for the infinite possibilities that life holds in store for us if we open our minds and let ourselves think outside our usual box.

I am grateful for life's myriad of choices, and for knowing I am always at choice even when I choose "whatever" which I rarely do.

Thank you, Spirit, for all the amazing roads with twists and turns that life offers! This is freedom. This is free will. And I am truly grateful.

I am in gratitude for the knowledge
that I don't need to (and couldn't anyway)
fix or change someone I love.
Instead, I feel a deep knowing that they
are on their own perfect right path.

No matter where they are, I see them as
perfect, whole and complete
which is the Truth of each of us
at our core.

I use my energy in fixing myself!

Knowing I am a work in progress, and that
each and every day, I am getting better
and better.

Thank you, Life!

There is beauty and magic to be found in waking up at dawn.

I am grateful for waking up early, for the serenity and quiet peace
I am greeted with each morning;
for the cool refreshing morning air on hot summer days;
for the feeling of spacious time before my workday begins;
for my steady commitment to my spiritual practice, reading from deep pools of wisdom – and feeling that deep pool of wisdom within myself each morning
as I meditate, and connect with Spirit to start my day.

Truly thankful!

DEBORAH PERDUE

I am thankful that as I have matured,
I have become the kind of person who
reaches out, when someone I know speaks
of being in distress.

I feel fulfilled when I am able to be there
for somebody else, listening deeply,
and not trying to fix like I used to when I
played caretaker for others.

And I am also so grateful to be there
for myself.

I love myself, I love others,
I love the world!

GRACE *of* GRATITUDE REFLECTIONS

On the eve of Independence Day,
I am so grateful to live in the United States
with the true freedom we have,
individually and collectively.

We are free enough to disagree
and to bicker...
We are free enough to create
amazing innovations...
We are free enough to live the way
we choose to live
in such diverse ways.

I know how lucky I am, and we are,
to be here,
and I am grateful.

Today I am grateful for watching the
process of creation happen in my life,
from dream to sweet reality.
To set a goal or intent, and then to move
forward to help make it happen...

Sometimes the process takes longer
than I wish, and I get impatient
but if I do everything I can to manifest
the vision
and then sit back and wait, feeling
confident it will come to pass,
the results are very exciting
to eventually witness!

I know that the universe DOES conspire
to support what we commit to.
I am so thankful that this is so.

GRACE *of* GRATITUDE REFLECTIONS

It is another beautiful summer day,
filled with bright promise.
I love my life!

I am so grateful for my inner light
and love.

I am so grateful for beauty that abounds
in this world.

Contentment and peace reign.
Ahhhhh!

I am thankful for more equality,
justice and compassion for all.

I take the high road of optimism about
these tendencies in our society,
and I am profoundly grateful that cultural
change, though amazingly slow,
does prevail.

GRACE of GRATITUDE REFLECTIONS

"Let us be grateful to the people who make us happy; they are the charming gardeners who make our souls blossom."
– Marcel Proust

Today, I am so thankful for friends, for the
people who love me no matter what;
for the ones who are so close to me that
they barely notice the outside me,
because they know and understand and
love the inside me so much.

Ever-accepting, available when times
are tough, who will listen and counsel me
gently when it is needed and asked for.
And these special friends are ready to
share monumental occasions, and to
celebrate times of fun and joy
and laughter too!

Friends are our family that we choose, and
I appreciate each one,
from all the various paths of my life.

In the middle of a heatwave,
with temps at 100 degrees plus
I am so grateful for
the cool, clear, deep rivers nearby...
how blessed I am to live in Oregon!

I am thankful for my lifelong love
of swimming
for the weightlessness of floating
for the constant, soothing sound of the
river flowing
watching the birds flying by
in a deep blue sky
amidst a plethora of trees
in this paradise of Southern Oregon
countryside.

I am thankful for
relaxation and peace and joy and bliss
and quenching water!

Grace of Gratitude Reflections

Simply thankful for my charmed and
beautiful life.
I am grateful for those I love, both family
and friends, and for every being on this
earth, all doing their very best
even when my point of view
or lifestyle differs.

I am grateful for this sturdy body which
houses my soul...

and so thankful for all creatures great and
small; especially, right now, for tiny
hovering hummingbirds
visiting a newly-hung feeder;
for every blade of grass and every flower
for all the forests, lakes and oceans...

Beauty abounds.
Love abounds.
Peace abounds.

Thank you, Spirit!

Deborah Perdue

You know how sometimes things go wrong
and then you (or in this case me) are very
disappointed and dismayed?
When things happen where I am let down,
I can feel hopeless, as if there is a big
blockade in front of me.

What I am grateful for is how when
roadblocks happens in my life,
(after I go through the process of
disappointment, letting myself feel grief
about what didn't happen the way
I thought), then like a Phoenix, I DO rise
from the ashes, filled with new energy and
enthusiasm and motivation
to try try again!

I am thankful for my stick-to-it-ness!

So thankful for my sublime and sweet life
for relaxing into the flow,
unhurried
for feeling calm and peaceful and joyful
all combined
for the long summer hours of sunshine

LIFE IS GOOD!

DEBORAH PERDUE

I am so grateful for my high resolve;
to let what I know to be true really sink
into my consciousness;
to be filled with faith and trust in my life,
knowing I am truly guided
and supported always,
to lay fear and worry
and doubts aside.

All is well and I know it!

Thank you, God-Goddess-All That Is

I am thankful to be a work in progress.
I realize I don't know everything, and that
I am getting better and better each
and every day.
If I make a mistake, I can simply
course-correct.

And the universe is a work in progress, too!

It is constantly changing, evolving,
expanding.
And so am I!

Thankful for new ways of thinking,
new possibilities, unlimited choices.

As I realize tired old ways of thought
are no longer working,
I open my heart and mind up to the new.

I take the plunge into the unknown,
diving in,
courageous and brave.

I choose again!

Life gives us so much opportunity to grow
and change
and I am deeply grateful.

GRACE *of* GRATITUDE REFLECTIONS

*"I would rather be a superb meteor, every atom of me in magnificent glow,
than a sleepy and permanent planet....
I shall not waste my days in trying to prolong them. I shall use my time."*
Jack London

So grateful for the shining light that I am, and that we all truly are!

Let me remember to forge ahead with the new, to take chances and risks sometimes charting territory in the unknown,
so that I shine ever-brighter in my life expansion.

I am thankful to know that my aim is true...and that I am a beneficial presence in this world –
light-filled and spiritually strong!

I am grateful for the connection I almost always feel with Spirit,
that cannot go away or be halted unless I turn away from the Oneness
that is always there and let myself feel separate and alone
which I am not.

I recognize that I am ever-connected with my Source,
and I know it and feel it on deep levels today!

So thankful.

Today I celebrate the harmonious feeling
of thankfulness.

Gratitude raises my vibration, and is such a
powerful spiritual tool to uplevel every
moment of my life.

It sounds so simple and it is,
all I have to do is remember to go there!

Thank you, thank you, thank you, Life –
for every gift and blessing, large and small,
far and near – infinite gratitude for all!

Have you ever heard of the acronym
for FEAR:
False Evidence Appearing Real?

I am so thankful for getting out of fear's
grip quickly
when I get sucked in.

When I am in fear, it's almost never based
on what is true,
and I am filled with gratitude for
discernment in these matters.

So thankful for easy-goingness
for not pushing
for the natural flow of life
for lightness of being.

I am grateful for deep joy within me –
an infinite well.

"I open my heart to grace and bask in my Oneness with God."
from Unity's Daily Guides 6-3-15

The peace of God, the grace of God, the calm love of God is always within me.

It is almost beyond gratitude to know this is so – to feel it on such deep levels when I go within.

No matter what is happening on this Earth, outside me, I can always choose to go within and bask in the grace of God.

For this and so much more, I am thankful.

GRACE *of* GRATITUDE REFLECTIONS

Life is a multi-faceted jewel – and from
every facet shines a quality of Spirit
to behold and appreciate.

I am so grateful for each facet as I turn my
attention to it, it sparkles and comes alive:
Truth, Wisdom, Beauty, Peace, Love,
Harmony, Wellbeing, Abundance
and on and on and on...

Each of us also a facet of Divinity –
precious and divine –
light-filled and dazzling
when we focus on the Good of Life
and there I focus now.

Thank you, Spirit, for the willingness and persistence to be able to break an almost lifelong pattern.

Being willing to read wise words on the subject, and apply the teachings to my life; being willing to look deep within, to be honest with myself and ferret out old beliefs that no longer serve me.

And I'm grateful for discipline (a word I've never liked) to change the pattern, by consistently applying better habits instead.

I am grateful beyond measure for this shift and transformation in my life!

I am so very thankful for peace, for
serenity, for the calm and comfort of my
life, and where I live.
My home is a quiet sanctuary.

And I am aware that the inner peace I feel
and can always access if I get still,
is essential so that I can fully appreciate
the beauty and solace of home.

So thankful for inner and outer peace.

DEBORAH PERDUE

I am thankful for my strong will
and determination.
I rise to the occasion when I set my mind
on an intention or goal.

And conversely, I am grateful when and if
an obstacle of some sort presents itself.
When the universe is not letting something
transpire easily, I listen and yield.

Thank you, God, for the Yin Yang
of balance, and for my ability
to pay attention.

I am simply thankful today for the shimmering trees in the wind, as a gentle breeze shakes and stirs all the leaves so that they sparkle and glisten with light.

This magical effect of nature reminds me of the beauty and majesty of the One Life that animates all.

Blessings of joy!

I am in gratitude for all the times I have glimpsed the realms that are beyond the veil – invisible but powerful.

So grateful for when I can see beyond the collective falsehoods we have come to believe.

I do get stuck in the phenomenal world's afflictions sometimes, yet more and more, I am able to peek behind the curtain, and know and feel the everlasting-ness of Life – summoning up the peace that resides always in my heart even when sad events occur, and realize that continuity and infinite grace don't ever really disappear.

I see and feel the love, light and beauty that shines on, and animates all of life.

Thank you, Spirit!

GRACE *of* GRATITUDE REFLECTIONS

I sometimes forget the power of standing strong in gratitude.

Today, I shout out to the world that I am grateful for every little thing
that is part of my life – for the unseen power of Spirit working through every person and every event.

I am thankful for the gifts of Spirit, found in everything, even apparent adversity.

I praise the Good and I get more!

Yes!

Deborah Perdue

> *"I am free in the Spirit...and I'm only here for love."*
> song lyrics by Rickie Byar Beckwith

Today I celebrate my freedom. As a human, I am filled with free will,
not bound by anything except my own self-imposed limits.
And I am free to choose again in every moment.

And I know that as a Divine expression of Spirit,
I am even freer....
because we are free in the Spirit
and freedom is boundless and infinite.

Deeply grateful for all the freedom I have and am in every way!

GRACE *of* GRATITUDE REFLECTIONS

In gratitude, I stand strong in my Faith
that the universe is benevolent
and I am always supported.

DEBORAH PERDUE

So thankful for my tenacity and courage.
I take brand new steps in my life,
and dare greatly.
Thank you, Spirit, for the qualities
within me that allow me
to step into unfamiliar territory,
with spunk.

I go forward in joy!

GRACE *of* GRATITUDE REFLECTIONS

Today I am acknowledging the deep
gratitude I have for creativity –
to the artists, authors and musicians who
touch into Spirit to express their gifts and
talents; through colors, textures, musical
notes and word play in delightful
and awe-inspiring ways.

And I toast creativity found in other areas
of our lives too – mathematicians,
scientists, parents, inspirational speakers,
teachers, entrepreneurs –
all are so creative, too.

And most of all, I am thankful to the
amazing creative urge of Mother Nature
that inspires me daily – seen in the spiral
galaxies, exploding stars,
sacred ancient redwood trees, diverse flora,
all creatures great and small,
and ever-changing rivers
and deep, deep oceans.

CREATIVITY ABOUNDS!

I am grateful for the times where life
takes a surprise twist and turn
and it doesn't feel good at first; it can even
feel devastating, if we lose a job, for
instance, or find out divorce is imminent…
we are shaken out of our routines or
comfort zone
but then later on, looking back,
it is so evident that Spirit had something
better in mind.

I am thankful for being open to change
and flowing with it, trusting that what's
around the corner is even better.

GRACE *of* GRATITUDE REFLECTIONS

*"We are never more than one grateful thought
away from peace of heart."*
David Steindl-Rast

Let me remember, always, to appreciate
the moment; being in gratitude for the
meeting of each new day
whatever is in store…

to say Thank You for all the blessings of my
life, simple and complex.

And there I will abide in that wondrous
space of peace of heart.

So thankful for moving forward, step by step, and not giving up even when I falter or get overwhelmed.

It doesn't matter if progress is slow, as long as I strive to reach a sought-after goal or intent.

In time, in perfect time, I get there.

And it's so ironic to look back later and see how relatively easy it was to get it done and to learn to be tender towards myself
for the amount of time
I spent ruminating about it rather than digging in to actually do it.

Onward & upward!

In gratitude, for the times I know within myself that I have done an amazing job, whether it is a public speaking event I was nervous about, or simply showing love and acceptance to someone when I thought I couldn't.

Or when I have intense focus and drive to get something challenging done that I feared would be much harder than it turned out to be.

And I don't need public acclaim or praise. I am grateful for my own appreciation of a job well-done, and for my own "attagirl."

I am so thankful for the person I am, and for all the gifts that are mine, as a divine spark of the One.

To let go of expectations is so important in life. If I feel that someone let me down, or an event or happening didn't go the way it should have gone, I am filled with temporary disappointment.

Instead, if I let go of expectations and go deep within to discover what there is to be grateful for, it naturally shifts
the situation to an exalted level, washing away a sense of unfulfillment.

So, I am grateful that I am vigilant in fueling gratitude, that I remember it even during unhappy times because
it is a potent tool to shift me into the enough-ness, into the bounty
of abundant joy and peace that is nourishment to the soul.

And I am grateful for gentle nudges from the Universe when needed,
to help me remember.

GRACE *of* GRATITUDE REFLECTIONS

I am so thankful for life everywhere
and in everything...
all is alive! The whole universe upon
universe is teeming with life...
in the expanse of the galaxies and cosmos
with zillions of stars
in the tiniest worlds, as in the particles and
waves at the core of everything
that scientists have discovered are dancing
and disappearing.

For life in people,
for life in all creatures great and small,
for life in all of nature,

Life flowing through me...
Life flowing through you...

Nothing ever dies, it simply transforms

Life is truly magical!
and I am deeply grateful

DEBORAH PERDUE

*"Frankly, happiness is overrated...
Happiness is one of a thousand feelings and
under it, and all the other human feelings,
is the depth of being alive."*
Mark Nepo

Today I am thankful for my ability to allow myself to feel all emotions...
to let them be with me when they are – not to run and hide. To be genuine, to be authentic, and to let disappointment or guilt or resentment be there in my heart when they need to be, knowing that just like happiness, they are fleeting and to deny them builds up armor in my heart.

So, I am grateful for a clear emotional field, facing all parts of my human self, and accepting it all.

I am perfect exactly as I am,
and also, exactly as I am not.

Hallelujah!

So thankful for spiritual evolution...
the way the world's peoples are becoming
more conscious of the Oneness
that is the Truth of our being.

We are waking up one by one
until there is a tipping point so that the
world can shift from war to peace,
from hatred to love,
from injustice to harmony.

Sometimes it doesn't seem possible
yet I know it is true.

And in my own life, I have watched my
own evolving and changing
to be more of a light in the world.

And I am deeply grateful.

Today I am thankful for the Dress
Rehearsals of life, where we are given a
chance to practice something
which may not yet come to fruition,
but the Universe has a plan, and it will.

Also grateful for do-overs,
and the constant chances we are given
to choose again.

Ain't life grand?!

GRACE *of* GRATITUDE REFLECTIONS

Have you ever thought about how much
there is to read during our lifetimes...
how much there is to do?!
Today I am grateful for all the plenty and
bountiful choices we have in this life; for
all the myriad of books, music, art, science,
math, spirituality, and history there is to
study and immerse myself in.

There is literally an infinity of avenues
to delve into!

Life is so rich.

WOW!

I acknowledge and appreciate the glorious beauty of the Springtime, with all its renewal, revitalization and regeneration.

Nature dresses up the trees in their verdant finery, and the green of the newborn grass is almost neon, and wildflowers keep emerging: right now white baby irises, soon magenta sweetpeas galore.

Spring reminds me of how the light always shines after a time of darkness; how from the bareness and grey of winter emerges the sparkling new!

And how in our own emotions, there are ups and downs, times of sorrow and grief, and then how it is always true that this, too, shall pass, and the light of gladness, the light of joy, the light of peace always shines again

ALL IS ALIVE!
ALL IS PART OF SPIRIT!
ALL IS MADE NEW!

GRACE *of* GRATITUDE REFLECTIONS

Tonight I am grateful for feeling lit up
and inspired!

I know as I open my mind and heart,
I light up others with how I shine.

And together, as more and more of us
shine, we transform our lives
for the better in unique and
wondrous ways!

Totally thankful.

DEBORAH PERDUE

Today, I am in deep gratitude for my
knowing and growing understanding
that all is One, that we all spring from the
same well of Spirit and so, we have at our
beck and call all that Spirit is....
to create Heaven on earth
as we so desire.

Thank you, Life!

GRACE *of* GRATITUDE REFLECTIONS

I am so grateful for perspective
and deep understanding.
When things seem unstable, when things
can seem dire or scary or uncertain,
I return to what I truly know about God
and life, and it calms me, it balances me,
it nurtures me.

For this knowing and remembering, and for
my ability to get there,
I am truly thankful.

And what I know is that life is good,
God is good –
at the core of life is peace and joy and bliss.

Being in the now transports me there.

I am thankful for ever-changing
temporal situations.
What was bothering me yesterday blows
away like a kite in the sky during a strong
prevailing wind
away away away!

So grateful for the unchanging peace and
joy and serenity,
that is always found within,
when I let myself go there.

Thank you, God

Thankful for close friends, who can be confided in and sometimes vented to, who listen with a caring non-judgmental ear when needed, and offer ideas and solutions that I can take or leave.

How amazing to be understood and unconditionally loved by another fellow human being in times of stress. And, also to celebrate together in good times.

Today I am deeply grateful for the giving and receiving of a long-standing friendship!

So grateful for old-story longtime karmic
patterns changing –
for watching and enjoying a beneficial,
intended change take place in my life.

I know that anything we want to shift can
be shifted, and that we have the power
and the strength and the motivation
to make a shift
with Spirit supporting and guiding us
as it always does.

Deeply thankful!

Grace of Gratitude Reflections

So grateful for the wisdom handed down
from the ages – the teachings that are
open and accepting of all –
that teach there is Oneness in
and through everyone and everything.
I am thankful science is revealing
this too.

I celebrate the open, accepting, loving,
forgiveness that comes so easily to those
who are truly enlightened –
Christ's teachings in their purest form.

And I am thankful for my own openness to
receive the wisdom through the ages
to be a bright light in a world that seems
not to understand the intrinsic oneness
of all.

As each of us opens our minds and realizes
the Divinity within everything,
the world does change in beneficial ways.

Deborah Perdue

> "I speak the desires of my heart
> and then I let them go."
> From Unity's *Daily Word*, April 17, 2015

It is new for me to be detached from a solution in life – to let Spirit do its great work and let go, knowing that I don't need to concern myself with the details of HOW an intention will come to pass.

Certainly, I do what I can to help manifest an idea or what I intend, but I see more and more that pushing or forcing is fruitless and can, in fact, get in the way.

I am so thankful for discovering that
letting go IS beneficial
and I open my arms and heart wide
to let new, exciting opportunities arise,
even more delightful than
my wildest dreams!

GRACE *of* GRATITUDE REFLECTIONS

Today I give thanks for my strong and able
body; for my health and well-being;
for every part of all the systems that work
automatically. Our bodies are a miracle
and a mini cosmos!

Thank you, Spirit, for my breath,
my circulation,
for my strength and flexibility...
for smiles and sighs,
laughter and tears,
for hiccups!
for walks in nature...
for dancing and running,
for making love

for seeing and smelling and touching and
hearing and tasting

for all that my body allows me to do
in this world

It is truly a blessed vessel for my soul,
and I am so thankful.

When the bank account gets low, I turn to
all the magnificent abundance
and prosperity that is always flooding
into my life:
friends galore, loving, comfy home life,
immersed in beautiful nature,
creativity abounds.
Gifts from the universe in so many ways
present themselves.
And then I remember how I AM
prosperous, my life is abundant
and I am free!

I am deeply grateful for the ability to focus
on what is right!

Today I shine God's Love and Light from
my heart to the world!
And I am so thankful for the healing
power of Love

I know that the love of God is omnipotent
and when I open my heart, I embody that
powerful love which casts everything in
the light of wonder and beauty.

I am grateful for love of all kinds –
for self-love which is the bridge to love
others; and for the love I share with family,
and with friends;
for the love I have in my heart for all
people, all animals, all of nature,
everything!

As I open my heart more and more,
love rules my life.

Deborah Perdue

> *"Walk as if you are kissing the Earth with your feet."*
> Thich Nhat Hanh

Thank you, Mother Nature, for all the glory and bounty that are the trees, the rivers, the oceans, the skies, the silence of the natural world. It is pure joy to walk in a nearby park, with the sounds of the river flowing, with newly budding leaves and wildflowers everywhere I look this time of year.
I am awestruck at the beauty of this earth, and daily walks keep me grounded in all that nature provides us.

I am grateful to live in the country, with an infinity of trees and mountains and wildlife. I am grateful to kiss the earth with my feet, and to be in the Now and let worries and anxiety go.

And I am grateful for Spirit who creates it all, and that Spirit is also within me. How good is that?!

Grace *of* Gratitude Reflections

"I know that the changeless abides within me. I am calm and peaceful in the midst of confusion. I know that nothing disturbs the soul. Peace, infinite peace, is at the center of my being."

Ernest Holmes

I am thankful for the changeless, the invisible and unseen that is always there, back of everything.
It is always accessible to me when I pause to have a "timeout" and go within.

What holds me together when my stable world gets rocked by a seismic shift, is the knowing, remembering and connecting to the Truth of me, to the Truth of all life, which is that we are eternal beings, and it helps to remember "This, too, shall pass" and guess what?
It always does.

Thank you, Spirit, within and all around!

Deborah Perdue

"The same stream of life that runs through my veins night and day runs through the world and dances in rhythmic measures."
Rabindranath Tagore

I am grateful beyond measure for the unseen architecture of life.
Thankful for everything that is not visible to our human eyes, but is part of an intricate, invisible structure that fortifies and animates all life.

And I'm talking about powerful forces like love, sweet love –
and peace, compassion, freedom, joy, intuition, chakras, will, cooperation, harmony, and receptivity, to name a few.

And then there are the invisible dimensions, the realms behind the veil.

We feel all this from within, although we can't tangibly see any of it.
For this and so much more, I am thankful!

GRACE *of* GRATITUDE REFLECTIONS

So thankful for surprises – a heartfelt note
of appreciation in my email box in the
morning; a surprise greeting card signed by
my husband and the pups;
lilacs in abundance, newfound energy
within me to clear and clean.....

I am grateful for all that life
has in store for me,
for the sweet surprises that greet me each
and every day.

And that includes my own daring to step
out into the unknown,
and allow for astonishing new expansion.

Deborah Perdue

I am so thankful for a stable home
life…filled with love and security
with a giving and receiving
that is balanced
and deep sharing and caring
for each other.

Comfortable routines…
a home base to be counted on
are so appreciated…

and puppy dogs, too!

Life is good!

I am thankful for today, right now, this exact moment...
Because this moment, this present moment, is really all there is
and it is perfect just as it is,
and just as it is not.

Deeply grateful for feeling and experiencing the right here right now
when I don't get swept away
by the past or the future.

Be here now.

I trust completely
in the Good of the Universe
as I allow myself to relax into the
assurance of Trust and Peace, and
celebrate the feeling of Freedom
that naturally follows.

For this and so much more,
I am grateful.

GRACE *of* GRATITUDE REFLECTIONS

I am continually thankful for the coming of Spring – the beauty so stunning and spectacular! I am grateful for the warmth of the sun that relaxes and mellows my body, heart and soul;
for the profusion of wildflowers; the wind blowing newborn grass; the dramatic big clouds in the bright blue sky...

All of this soothes my spirit as the light keeps lengthening the days.

Nature with its clockwork timing is nothing short of miraculous.

Life is miraculous!

I am deeply grateful.

Amen.

DEBORAH PERDUE

So grateful to hear, acknowledge and most importantly, LISTEN,
to my inner voice of guidance.

I let the busyness of life subside, tuning in to hear the still, small voice within which clearly guides me.

I hone my skill and willingness to listen.

That which is mine to do is shown to me, and I pay attention and do it!

Thank you, Spirit.

GRACE *of* GRATITUDE REFLECTIONS

I am thankful for simplicity,
for not over-thinking,
for easy peace and joy and grace.

I take time each day to play, to ground
myself in Mother Earth, to appreciate the
simple things in life.

And I am ever grateful.

DEBORAH PERDUE

We are literally stardust!

What a magical, mystical life this is.

I am so grateful to be an integral part of life, a unique and essential part of the Divine, and deeply aware of my connection to the stars and the earth and the sky and all of life!

GRACE *of* GRATITUDE REFLECTIONS

Used to be that I stuffed my feelings or
denied them. Not anymore!

I am grateful to let all feelings out, whether
seemingly positive or "negative."
Each one is valid, and is deserving
of being felt.

Feelings shift and change, and do not stick
around if they are acknowledged.
And they do have a lesson for me,
if I listen.

I am thankful for this awareness,
and for listening!

DEBORAH PERDUE

I am grateful for the ability to think
outside the box...
to find a new solution when something is
not working well anymore.

I am thankful for inspiration
and intuition
that guides me to new ideas!

Life is continually shifting and changing,
and I am thankful for my open mind and
open heart to let the new come in.

"Patience is natural to those who trust."
from A Course in Miracles

Sometimes I get so impatient, I want everything to happen NOW!
At times, I just don't understand delay and waiting.
And this morning, in my prayer and meditation time, I got clear guidance to practice
P A T I E N C E.

So, knowing that there is always divine right timing, I relax into that knowing and rest assured that all is truly well.
I trust completely in the flow of life and the good of the universe.
And I am thankful.

DEBORAH PERDUE

"I can experience heaven here and now, for it is a state of mind always available to me."
from Unity's *Daily Word*, 3/19/15

I am so grateful for the heaven I can see, feel, and celebrate right here in this lifetime.

I am so grateful for all of life, and everything is alive!
For all creatures great and small,
for all of nature, for all the world's people,
for the galaxies and quarks and supernovas,
and most of all, for the unseen mystery of life that we can't quite fathom.

Thank you, Father-Mother God, for each part of creation.

And I create peace, love, joy, wonder, abundance and magic
with my thoughts today and tomorrow, ever-increasingly.

Thank you, Life, for the abundance and
plentitude of Nature...
where tiny stubborn plants crop up
between sidewalk cracks,
where spring cherry blossoms are blown in
the wind like snowflakes,
where the stars in the sky are so profuse we
cannot count them,
and there is not only one universe,
but universe upon universe,
stretching to infinity!

I am in deep gratitude for the awareness
I have of the beauty and wonder and
magic of life.

Thank you, Spirit, for my growing,
ever-evolving consciousness so that I am
able to grasp more of what is important in
life, and let go of what is not.

I am grateful to realize that everything
I experience comes from how I perceive it,
and I can always change my mind!

How powerful we truly are
when we let go of feeling like a victim
and let our true essence shine.

Thankful for my knowledge that moods
are always fleeting and changing...
they don't stay, they are always on the
move like clouds blown by the wind
in the sky...

so when i am feeling a little down,
I know that soon I will be back into the
vibration of peace and more joy,
and that my gratitude practice
always helps!

Deeply grateful.

Today I turn away from
worry, fear and doubt.
They do not serve me, and I let them go.

Instead, I focus on the magical, mystical
qualities of life that are the true reality.

I put my trust and faith in the Good.

I appreciate the love, abundance, peace
and joy of Spirit –
and all of it expands!

GRACE *of* GRATITUDE REFLECTIONS

*"When your smile is sincere,
you are a smile millionaire."*
Paramahansa Yogananda

I have always been one of those people with a naturally optimistic attitude. Smiles and laughter come easily to me. I see the glass as half full rather than empty. I consider myself very fortunate to have not ever suffered long-standing depression.

Thank you, Spirit, for the gift of joy that is a natural wellspring within me.

So thankful for keeping things simple
and for watching how there truly is
divine right order and timing,
if I quit stressing and simply allow!

GRACE *of* GRATITUDE REFLECTIONS

Thank you, Spirit, for the love and light
that fills universe upon universe,
stretching out to infinity.

Love and light is truly all that matters;
snuffing out darkness; and permeating
each being's heart and soul
if, and when, they let themselves
recognize it.

I am grateful for the expanding love and
light that is the truth of me,
and that I know it.

Today, on Martin Luther King Jr. Day,
I feel great gratitude in my heart for the peacemakers of this world.

I am thankful for those who have stood up for peace and equality and justice and love often at great cost to themselves.....

For others, too, such as Mahatma Ghandi and Mother Teresa
who in selfless ways, have changed the world for the better.

And for those who take a stand every day in their own hearts and minds for peace and love and live it to the best of their abilities, despite apparent unrest and hatred and divisiveness.

Let peace prevail...

GRACE *of* GRATITUDE REFLECTIONS

Thank you, Spirit,
for the infinite nature of life.

I am grateful for the microcosms,
teeny tiny worlds such as the cells and
particles dancing and disappearing
within us and all sentient beings.
I appreciate the grains of sand, life
underground, even the ants and their
doings, the sea water teeming with tiny life…

And I am grateful for the macrocosms,
huge, gigantic worlds like giant stars and
black holes; the zillions of stars in the sky;
suns and moons and planets galore.

And here we are –
an integral part of all of it!

I am so thankful for the infinity of Life
and for all parts of it, seen and unseen.
It is truly magic

WOW!

Deborah Perdue teaches spiritual classes, and facilitates workshops and retreats on the topics of gratitude, abundance and how to live a life of joy. As well as authoring several books, she publishes blogs and articles on inner peace and gratitude. Deborah has been a licensed practitioner for the Centers for Spiritual Living since 2006. She lives in beautiful Southern Oregon on five acres with her husband and menagerie.

It is her calling and intention to continue to expand the potent spiritual practice of gratitude in the world!

GO TO

www.graceofgratitude.com

to sign up for Daily Gratitude Affirmations (like these), or to order
more products including Gratitude Journals, coloring books and beautiful greeting cards.

If you enjoyed this book, please take a moment to let other people know by posting a review on amazon.com.
Thank you.

If you would like to be on our email list to hear of new products
and other news, or simply to communicate with us, please email
info@graceofgratitude.com

www.ingramcontent.com/pod-product-compliance
Lightning Source LLC
Chambersburg PA
CBHW050602300426
44112CB00013B/2031